SCHOLASTIC

25 Best-Ever
Collaborative
Books for Young Writers

Ready-to-Use Templates to Help Develop Early Writing Skills and Meet the Common Core State Standards

Susan Stroeher

New York • Toronto • London • Auckland • Sydney
Mexico City • New Delhi • Hong Kong • Buenos Aires

Teaching
Resources

Scholastic Inc. grants teachers permission to photocopy the reproducible pages from this book for classroom use. Purchase of this book entitles use of reproducibles by one teacher for one classroom only. No other part of this publication may be reproduced in whole or in part, or stored in a retrieval system, or transmitted in any form or by any means, electronic, mechanical, photocopying, recording, or otherwise, without written permission of the publisher. For information regarding permission, write to Scholastic Inc., 557 Broadway, New York, NY 10012.

Editor: Maria L. Chang
Designer: Holly Grundon
Illustrations: Susan Stroeher

ISBN: 978-0-545-20716-4
Copyright © 2012 by Susan Stroeher
All rights reserved.
Printed in the U.S.A.

1 2 3 4 5 6 7 8 9 10   40   19 18 17 16 15 14 13 12

Contents

Introduction

Teachers of early learners have the privilege of watching children develop into independent writers and readers. This process can be equally exciting for each child as his or her skills mature and he or she experiences success as an emerging reader and writer. As educators of young students, we have the benefit of witnessing their unbridled enthusiasm and thirst for learning. If we are mindful to engage kids on their level, we can ensure their continued progress. Offering children a variety of appealing writing opportunities increases their motivation, and their excitement can spread like wildfire in a primary classroom.

25 Best-Ever Collaborative Books for Young Writers features several writing opportunities that will greatly enhance your class's writing repertoire as well as motivate and excite your budding authors. Titles and assignments are geared toward children in Grades K–2, and modifications can easily be made to target your specific student population. Assignments involve writing and illustrating in response to a prompt or theme. Regardless of children's abilities, these assignments are designed to encourage and celebrate individual writing. Children share their completed work with the class, providing them with valuable writing, reading, and speaking practice as well as giving them a sense of accomplishment when they receive immediate feedback from their teacher and classmates. Individual student accountability is another component in which children rise to expectations and gain practice assessing their work. Collect and assemble finished pages into three-ring binders and display these collaborative books in your classroom library to document students' growth as writers.

What's Inside

All the titles in this collection are easy to implement and require little effort from you, the teacher. Each comes with a teacher page or a parent letter that explains the writing assignment, reproducible cover and interior templates, and occasionally custom clip art or samples. Fun, creative prompts are designed to engage children on both a personal and an academic level. Choose from 25 titles that appeal to your student population and/or support your units of study. The titles fall under three categories.

Take-Home Class Journals – All journals (in the form of 1/2-inch, three-ring binders) travel back and forth between home and school, and children complete the assignments at home. This valuable home component not only reinforces the classroom instruction, but also gives parents a front-row seat in their child's progress. Parents are strongly encouraged to help with their children's writing. Once completed, the journals are returned to the classroom, and children read and share their entry, giving them a reading and speaking opportunity.

Individual Shape Books – Shape books give every child a chance to publish his or her own individual book. The shapes coincide with the writing topics, and finished books are usually four to five pages in length. Shape books require classroom time, often a week, to complete. Writing and illustrating is the focus of every page. These books serve as valuable performance assessments and provide authentic documentation of student work. When finished, display shape books in the classroom or present them as treasured keepsakes to parents during conference time.

Collaborative Class Books – These books are created by and belong to the entire class. Every child contributes one page to collectively produce a book. A writing prompt initiates the assignment, and each child writes and illustrates a response on his or her individual page. Student pages can usually be completed within a day or two, and then collected and assembled in a 1/2-inch, three-ring binder to create the class book. Once a book is complete, invite young authors to share and celebrate every entry. Then proudly display this latest publication in your classroom library.

Building Writing Skills

If possible, introduce the journals on the first week of school. The beauty of these writing assignments is that they are appropriate for all children, regardless of their writing ability. No matter where a child falls developmentally, he or she can successfully complete these assignments and feel encouraged and proud of his or her final product. In addition, these writing assignments are designed to meet the Common Core State Standards (page 8).

Keep in mind that writing is a newfound skill at the primary level, and children are excited to write in any capacity because it's so new. Writing interventions—such as dictating, labeling, tracing, copying, or sounding out words—are all accepted and encouraged. In some cases, solely illustrating a response is an appropriate option. The assignments still reinforce written communication and, with each completed entry, children gain experience and growth.

Suggestions for differentiated instruction are sometimes included. You might need to adapt and individualize templates for children by adding or omitting lines, dotting letters or words, or reducing the amount of writing with various sentence starters. Consider your class population and modify the given templates and assignments to best serve individuals. Keeping the process fun, non-threatening, and celebratory will help your students grow into successful writers and readers.

Involving Parents

Get parents involved in the writing process from the very beginning. Back-to-School Night is ideal for introducing families to the numerous writing assignments they will see throughout the year. This is helpful especially for the Take-Home Journals, as parents will be directly involved in their completion. Pass around the journals (if you have some ready) and show sample entries to help families understand their role in this process. In the days preceding or following Back-to-School Night, send home the parent/family letter that introduces the Take-Home Journals and explains the families' expected participation. (Make double-sided copies of pages 9 and 10.)

If possible, outline and demonstrate to parents the writing strategies used in the classroom, and encourage parents to use them at home. Include a laminated copy of the Writing Strategies handout (page 10) in each Take-Home Journal, after the parent letter. This way, parents can refer to it while writing with their child. Alternatively, you might hold a separate parents workshop that is completely devoted to teaching writing strategies. Most importantly, emphasize the "celebratory approach" parents should take when writing with their children.

Weekly or monthly communication to families is the perfect venue for announcing the completion of Collaborative Class Books or Individual Shape Books. If a new Take-Home Journal has been launched and is beginning to circulate among children, be sure to inform parents in order to minimize confusion when their turn comes. Always make all these collaborative books available in your classroom library for parents to browse.

Incorporating Artwork

Illustrating is a serious component of these writing assignments. Artwork enhances the final piece, provides a creative outlet, supports the text (if done correctly), and helps develop fine-motor skills. For many children who are not yet capable of writing, the illustration is the only written documentation of their work. Make it equally important as writing by specifying artistic expectations and holding children accountable for doing their best work.

"Five or more colors" is the primary expectation. This might appear trivial, but it actually sets the bar for future work habits and study skills. It also keeps children accountable for their completed work as they can't turn it in unless five different colors have been counted. Consider using only colored pencils and crayons. These work fine-motor muscles more effectively than markers. Children have to press really hard and color extensively to fill a space with a colored pencil versus with a marker. Markers are often limited in their color collection, bleed through paper, and eventually dry out, providing inconsistent coverage. For special illustrations, however, try outlining drawings in black permanent marker to give them great definition. Coloring these outlined pictures tends to be more successful as illustrations are compartmentalized for children.

Encourage adequate detail in children's drawings. Every writing assignment requires children to recount authentic or fictional stories involving themselves, so they must depict themselves with self-portraits. Specify six details on self-portraits, such as eyelashes, ears, freckles, patterns on clothes, and five fingers. Help reluctant artists get comfortable by frequently modeling the sequence for drawing a person (see above). Alter the modeling by sometimes drawing a boy, sometimes a girl, short hair, long hair, various details, and so on.

Cutting: When cutting out the cover and interior templates, always leave a margin of white around the perimeter of every piece. Do not cut directly on the solid black line. This perimeter of white space helps better define the artwork and makes for a more consistent look. Many templates and samples throughout the book are outlined in black and bordered by a dotted line. These dotted lines serve as a guide as you cut out items. Cut in between the solid black line of the template and the dotted lines.

Rubrics and Expectations

Holding children accountable for their work is critical to their future success. Consistent expectations will train children to assess their work and determine if it's adequately completed. Early primary students can be responsible for quality work and following directions when you make your expectations clear.

The list of age-appropriate criteria below can help clarify expectations for children. Each one is illustrated on the rubric (page 11) so children can successfully read them. Invite children to assess their work by drawing a happy, straight, or sad face in the first column of circles provided. You can use the second column of circles for your own assessment of completed work, too.

1. Name – The child's name is included on the work and is written correctly, with an uppercase letter followed by lowercase letters. Handwriting is neat.

2. Date – The date is written on the assignment.

3. Five or more colors – Completed illustrations must include five or more colors. Coloring is neat and time has obviously been devoted to the final product.

4. Best work – The child considers the work to be his or her best effort. Encourage children to ask themselves, "Is there anything I can add to make this even better? Is this my neatest work?"

5. Sound out words by myself – Certain assignments require a performance assessment so you can see where a child is developmentally. In such cases, remind children that writing should be done without assistance from the teacher or classmates.

6. Adequate detail – The child includes appropriate detail in his or her written and illustrated work.

7. Ending punctuation – Sentences end either with a period, question mark, or exclamation point.

8. Finger spacing – There is appropriate (finger) space between words.

9. Correct use of uppercase letters – The first letter in every sentence is written with an uppercase (capital) letter, and the remaining letters are lowercase.

10. Labeling – Two or three things are labeled in the child's illustrations.

11. Picture matches text – Children should check that the completed illustration adds to the clarity of the text and that the words and picture convey the same message.

Don't feel it's necessary to use all the criteria at once. Feel free to copy and cut apart the page to create your own custom rubric. Pick and choose different expectations, depending on the assignment, and slowly add more as the year progresses and children mature.

End of the Year

At the end of the year, dismantle your journals and class books and sort individual entries for each child. Many student entries are on standard letter-size paper, so consider compiling them in individual 1/2-inch, three-ring binders of their own. (Include 1/2-inch, three-ring binders with transparent slipcovers on your school supply list.) This portfolio of work is a great keepsake and documentation of children's academic progress. While sorting through the journals, select the best of the best and make color copies so you can use them as models the following year when you introduce these titles to new students and families.

No matter how many titles you decide to incorporate into your writing program, your students will benefit from the writing exposure, artistic process, and sense of accomplishment. Happy writing!

Common Core State Standards in Writing and Language

The writing assignments in this book are designed to meet the following Common Core State Standards for writing and language in the primary grades.

	Kindergarten	Grade 1	Grade 2
Text Types and Purposes	**W.K.1** Use a combination of drawing, dictating, and writing to compose opinion pieces in which they tell a reader the topic or the name of the book they are writing about and state an opinion or preference about the topic or book (e.g., *My favorite book is …*). **W.K.2** Use a combination of drawing, dictating, and writing to compose informative/explanatory texts in which they name what they are writing about and supply some information about the topic. **W.K.3** Use a combination of drawing, dictating, and writing to narrate a single event or several loosely linked events, tell about the events in the order in which they occurred, and provide a reaction to what happened.	**W.1.1** Write opinion pieces in which they introduce the topic or name the book they are writing about, state an opinion, supply a reason for the opinion, and provide some sense of closure. **W.1.2** Write informative/explanatory texts in which they name a topic, supply some facts about the topic, and provide some sense of closure. **W.1.3** Write narratives in which they recount two or more appropriately sequenced events, include some details regarding what happened, use temporal words to signal event order, and provide some sense of closure.	**W.2.1** Write opinion pieces in which they introduce the topic or book they are writing about, state an opinion, supply reasons that support the opinion, use linking words (e.g., *because, and, also*) to connect opinion and reasons, and provide a concluding statement or section. **W.2.2** Write informative/explanatory texts in which they introduce a topic, use facts and definitions to develop points, and provide a concluding statement or section. **W.2.3** Write narratives in which they recount a well-elaborated event or short sequence of events, include details to describe actions, thoughts, and feelings, use temporal words to signal event order, and provide a sense of closure.
Production and Distribution of Writing	**W.K.5.** With guidance and support from adults, respond to questions and suggestions from peers and add details to strengthen writing as needed. **W.K.6.** With guidance and support from adults, explore a variety of digital tools to produce and publish writing, including in collaboration with peers.	**W.1.5** With guidance and support from adults, focus on a topic, respond to questions and suggestions from peers, and add details to strengthen writing as needed. **W.1.6** With guidance and support from adults, use a variety of digital tools to produce and publish writing, including in collaboration with peers.	**W.2.5** With guidance and support from adults and peers, focus on a topic and strengthen writing as needed by revising and editing. **W.2.6** With guidance and support from adults, use a variety of digital tools to produce and publish writing, including in collaboration with peers.
Research to Build and Present Knowledge	**W.K.7** Participate in shared research and writing projects (e.g., explore a number of books by a favorite author and express opinions about them). **W.K.8** With guidance and support from adults, recall information from experiences or gather information from provided sources to answer a question.	**W.1.7** Participate in shared research and writing projects (e.g., explore a number of "how-to" books on a given topic and use them to write a sequence of instructions). **W.1.8** With guidance and support from adults, recall information from experiences or gather information from provided sources to answer a question.	**W.2.7** Participate in shared research and writing projects (e.g., read a number of books on a single topic to produce a report; record science observations). **W.2.8** Recall information from experiences or gather information from provided sources to answer a question.
Conventions of Standard English	**L.K.1** Demonstrate command of the conventions of standard English and grammar and usage when writing or speaking. **L.K.2** Demonstrate command of the conventions of standard English capitalization, punctuation, and spelling when writing.	**L.1.1** Demonstrate command of the conventions of standard English and grammar and usage when writing or speaking. **L.1.2** Demonstrate command of the conventions of standard English capitalization, punctuation, and spelling when writing.	**L.2.1** Demonstrate command of the conventions of standard English and grammar and usage when writing or speaking. **L.2.2** Demonstrate command of the conventions of standard English capitalization, punctuation, and spelling when writing.
Knowledge of Language			**L.2.3** Use knowledge of language and its conventions when writing, speaking, reading, or listening.

Source: Common Core State Standards Initiative http://www.corestandards.org/the-standards

25 Best-Ever Collaborative Books for Young Writers

Parent Letter

Dear Parents and Families:

Get ready to write! Your child is just discovering his or her newfound skill as a writer. This is an exciting time, and emerging writers are motivated to try new and varied writing opportunities.

In an effort to maintain this enthusiasm, we are offering a collection of Take-Home Journals that provide consistent writing practice in a motivating format. Titles and assignments are intentionally fun and appealing. Writing topics will range from imaginative to narrative, and a few titles will be math-related but still incorporate writing. Throughout the year, your help will be enlisted to assist your child in completing individual writing entries at home. This valuable home component will complement the classroom instruction and reinforce skills we are teaching.

Once completed, these entries will be shared (promoting speaking and reading skills), and children will field questions and comments from their peers. As the year progresses, our classroom library will grow. We encourage you to read through our journals as they find their way into your home. Enjoy the student entries, taking notice of the growth you will witness in our budding authors. At year's end, every journal will be dismantled and individual student entries will be compiled in 1/2-inch binders for each student to take home. You can look forward to an impressive body of work that will document personal growth and provide you with a wonderful keepsake you'll always treasure.

The remainder of this letter is a guideline to help you successfully write and mentor your child as you write together. First and foremost, keep all writing sessions fun and celebratory! The writing experience is meant to be a non-threatening one, in which children feel proud of their contribution and ultimately encouraged. Remember that children's writing abilities are different. Each child develops at his or her own rate, and this writing process is in constant flux and evolution. Your assistance will vary throughout the year as your child becomes more independent and less reliant on you. Use any of the writing strategies on the back of this page as you write with your child. Always keep your child's comfort level in mind and enjoy the process together.

Thank you in advance for your help!
Sincerely,

_____

Writing Strategies

As you write with your child throughout the year, your assistance will change as his or her writing matures. The writing strategies below cover a wide continuum of writing capabilities. All are age appropriate, practiced, and celebrated throughout their writing evolution. As you help your child, feel free to utilize any of the techniques below. Consult me if you need a demonstration or have any questions. Remember to keep the writing sessions encouraging and non-threatening.

Illustrations – Pictures convey messages and tell stories. Although illustrations are a requirement for each assignment, a child may choose solely to illustrate in lieu of writing. If your child isn't developmentally ready to write, illustrations are a precursor to the writing process. Pictures do convey a written message and eventually the pictures will coincide with written text.

Dictation – Your child may dictate his or her ideas and responses to you as you record them on paper.

Copying a response – Provide a written sentence (that your child dictates) so he or she can easily copy the words in his or her own handwriting. This provides great letter-writing practice.

Dotting out letters – You may dot out letters and words for your child to trace.

Beginning letter sounds – Emerging writers will start identifying the beginning letter sounds of words. Help your child stretch and isolate these beginning sounds so he or she can associate them with a letter. If letter recall is weak, provide an alphabet strip so your child can find the letter that matches the sound he or she hears. Your child can then record the letter, and you can write the remainder of the word or assist with further sounding out. Beginning writers start with mastering letter sounds and sequencing beginning, middle, and ending sounds in any given word. Sometimes isolating these various sounds is challenging for children. If they successfully hear the letter sound but don't know how to write that letter, provide your child with four or five possibilities and ask if he or she can identify the correct letter. Once successful at hearing beginning sounds, continued practice will progress into isolating ending sounds. This is an exciting stage of emerging writing!

Labeling – Once your child has mastered beginning letter sounds, labeling is a natural extension. A one- or two-word label is less intimidating than writing an entire sentence. The risk is taken away as your child "attacks" a word and attempts to hear and sequence the beginning, middle, and ending sounds to form a word (or label). Encourage multiple labels in your child's illustrations. This valuable practice boosts confidence!

Sounding out with assistance – Be present as your child writes and jump in when he or she struggles with a letter sound, letter recall, writing mechanics, spacing between words, isolating sounds, and so on. Always reinforce what they know and encourage their progress.

Independent writing – This is the ultimate goal! When your child is capable of writing independently, your job is to celebrate their success and congratulate them on a job well done. Don't be overly concerned with perfect spelling or punctuation mistakes. Gently point out editing suggestions but never to the point of deflating their enthusiasm.

Name

Date / /

5 or more colors

best work!

Cat ← sound out words by myself

or → adequate detail

. ? ! ending punctuation

finger spacing

The dog ran.

flower → label illustrations
bee

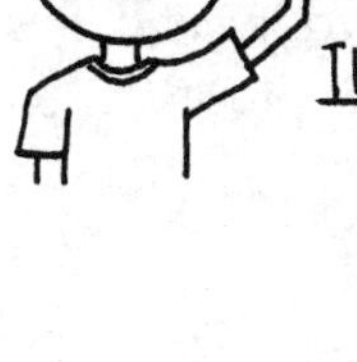

pictures match text

The boy was waving.

Take-Home Class Journals

This collection of 12 Take-Home Class Journals consists of ongoing titles that will circulate and recirculate the class on an as-needed basis, as well as one-time writing assignments that each child will get a turn to experience. Some of the journals, such as *Measurement Math* and *Number Cubes Math*, provide children with an opportunity to showcase their learning. Others will appeal to children because they can easily relate to the topics, which are centered on age-appropriate milestones. When a momentous event occurs in the life of a child, he or she will request that particular journal so a new entry can be completed and added to the class binder. Kids clamor for titles like *The "Ouch" Book*, *Tooth Tales*, and *The New Shoes Journal*. Significant life events, such as having a birthday or getting a haircut, are important to kids. They are motivated to write about them because they can't wait to share their big news.

Picture a child incessantly poking at your shoulder as he or she impatiently awaits your approval to share the news of their latest injury, a beloved pet, or a new haircut. This desire to share and communicate is now redirected to writing, reading, and speaking opportunities when they share their finished entry.

Conveniently, the opportunity to introduce most of these journals to the class will arise naturally. For example, it's almost a guarantee that a child will come off the playground on the first or second day of school and be hurt somehow. Use this opening to debut *The "Ouch" Book*. Gather the class and acknowledge the latest injury by presenting the injured student with the binder and a blank page to fill out. This journal will continuously travel back and forth between home and school all year long as children retell their stories of injuries, accidents, and mishaps. Because the journals travel home on an as-needed basis, it is conceivable that some children will have multiple entries in some journals and only one entry in others.

Parent Participation

Parent participation plays an integral role in the success of the Take-Home Class Journals. Communicating clear expectations is critical to each assignment's completion. Title-specific parent letters accompany every journal. These parent letters, strategically positioned on page one of the journals, provide a concise description of the assignment, outline writing and illustrating expectations, and detail writing strategies to aid in the parent/child writing process.

This home component, which involves parental help, is important. Not only does it allow reinforcement and additional practice at home, but it gives parents some perspective when they view the work of other classmates. Caution parents to keep in mind that every child develops at his or her own rate. Invite parents to come to you with any questions or concerns regarding their child.

Sign your parent letters and the journals' front covers from your class; for example, *By Mrs. Smith's Class.*

Management Tips

All journal covers are purposely sized for 8-1/2″ x 11″ paper so they easily slide into the cover pocket of a standard 1/2-inch, three-ring binder. Color the covers, then make extra color copies in case of loss or damage. Consider laminating these covers for durability. Even though cover pages will slide into the transparent slipcover of the binder, the lamination provides extra protection from spills and mishaps, extending the life of your purchase. Journals traveling between home and school hold up well in these sturdy binders. You may also want to photocopy the journals' interior pages onto card stock so they are less likely to pull out. Another option is to showcase completed entries in plastic page protectors.

Parent letters accompany every cover/title. These letters introduce the journal, explain the assignment, and provide logistical information for entry completion. Make double-sided copies of the parent letters so that the reverse side features the Writing Strategies handout (page 10) that details tips and interventions for writing with students at home. Place the parent letter—either in a plastic page protector or laminated and three-hole punched—at the front of the binder.

When sending a journal home with a student, place it in the child's backpack and give him or her a night or two to complete the entry. When the journal is brought back to school, invite the child to read and share his or her entry to classmates. Reward this sharing with a compliment, praise, and question time to foster a sense of accomplishment and satisfaction.

What If a Journal Doesn't Make It Back?

If you feel apprehensive at the thought of sending a journal home with a specific student and fear it will never return to school, make a copy of the parent letter and attach it to a blank interior page. This way the student can complete the writing assignment and insert his or her entry in the journal when the paper is returned to the classroom. Likewise, if multiple students request the same journal on the same day, this process allows for several students to participate simultaneously.

The Journals

Below is a list of the titles along with brief descriptions of the journals. A corresponding parent letter offers a more thorough explanation of each title.

1. **Weekend Pal** – The Weekend Pal is your class mascot (or stuffed animal). Every child in your class will take a turn bringing Weekend Pal home for a weekend and write and illustrate about their time together.

2. **Tooth Tales** – Anytime a tooth falls out, children will request this journal to chronicle their stories.

3. **The "Ouch" Book** – This ongoing collection chronicles every "owie," bump, scrape, and injury that happens to children in your class. This is the most-requested journal by far!

4. **The Birthday Book** – Birthdays are special because they happen just once a year. Children will recount their birthday fun in this journal. Invite children with summer birthdays to fill this one out in September.

5. **The New Shoes** – Children write and illustrate about the selection and purchase of their new shoes.

6. **The "New Do"** – Children write and illustrate about their latest haircuts or hairdos.

7. **Traveling Tales** – This journal is a progressive story in which every child adds on to the existing story.

8. **Class Reporter** – This journal challenges children to be resourceful as they recap a current article from the newspaper.

9. **The Question Journal** – Children will take turns answering and posing questions to one another.

10. **The Pet Journal** – Whether or not children have pets, they'll share their real or fictitious pet stories in this journal.

11. **Measurement Math Journal** – Students measure real household items with four different units of measurement (both standard and nonstandard) and record their findings in this journal.

12. **Number Cubes Math Journal** – Students roll three number cubes to get their total, and then search throughout their house to find the same number of a household item.

Dear Parents,

Your child's long-awaited turn with _____ , our "Weekend Pal," is finally here! Please welcome Weekend Pal into your home to join in all your weekend plans. (Just treat Weekend Pal like one of the family.) The pal should arrive with the following:

1. Weekend Pal journal
2. Two books to read together, titled:

   _____

   _____

3. Weekend Pal's backpack

Please be sure to keep track of Weekend Pal's belongings and return everything to school on Monday.

The Weekend Pal journal chronicles all of Weekend Pal's home visits. Have fun reading the previous entries, and then assist your child in recording his or her special weekend memories.

Locate the next empty page and instruct your child to illustrate and write about their adventures together. Make sure both your child and Weekend Pal are depicted in the illustration. Encourage five or more colors, lots of detail, and, as always, your child's best work. Labeling definitely adds to the final piece.

Depending on your child's writing capabilities, help as your child sounds out his or her account of the weekend. When school resumes next week, your child will share his or her entry with the class and respond to questions and comments. We look forward to hearing all about your weekend fun!

Thanks for your help and hospitality!

Sincerely,

_____

Weekend Pal

Name: _____ Date: _____

My Weekend with _____

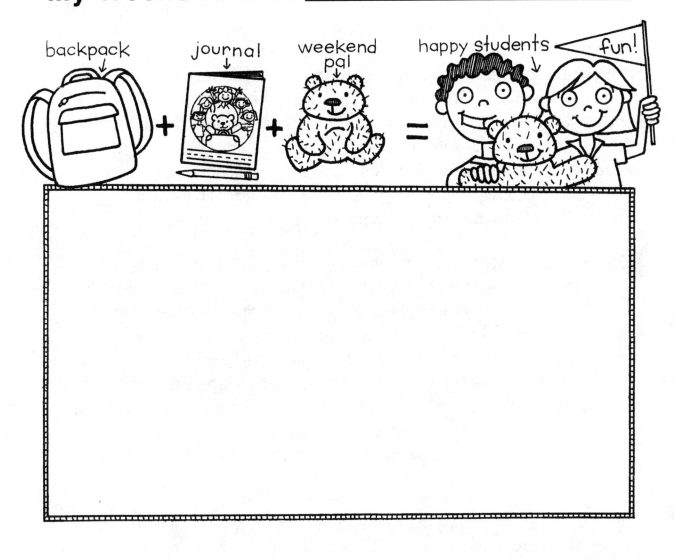

backpack   journal   weekend pal   happy students   fun!

_____

_____

_____

_____

Dear Parents,

Losing a tooth means an altered appearance, a visit from the Tooth Fairy, and exciting news. Sometimes a child has worked and wiggled a tooth for weeks before it finally comes out! Each lost tooth is equally exciting, and we want to hear all about it. Your child has requested the *Tooth Tales* journal so he or she can share the story of his or her missing tooth. Recount details of losing the tooth, such as how it came out, where and when it actually happened, the Tooth Fairy visit, and any other interesting information that enhance the story.

On the next empty page in the journal, invite your child to illustrate his or her story and write a brief sentence or two about the experience. Labeling the picture is always encouraged. Children are welcome to dictate to their parents, sound out words with the help of a parent or adult, or write independently. Whatever your child's writing capabilities, it's time to celebrate his or her attempt and encourage this writing entry. Illustrations should contain five or more colors, and neat handwriting is also an expectation. Please work in colored pencils or crayons as markers will likely bleed onto the next page. Colored pencils and crayons also offer more color variation.

Upon completion, return the journal to school so your child can read his or her entry to the class. All children can relate to this exciting experience. What a perfect venue to celebrate this exciting event and allow classmates to share in the enthusiasm!

Thanks for your assistance!

Sincerely,

_____

Tooth Tales

by

_____

- -

_____

Name: _____   Date: _____

I lost a tooth!

_____

_____

_____

_____

_____

Dear Parents,

Getting hurt is huge news in the life of any child. Children clamor to share their personal stories with teachers and classmates. *The "Ouch" Book* offers an opportunity to do just that in a written format. It is a perfect way to detail mishaps, accidents, injuries, and so on; receive empathy from friends; and provide valuable writing, illustrating, and speaking practice. Any "owie"—from a paper cut to stitches—is worthy of an entry in *The "Ouch" Book*.

Enjoy reading the prior entries, and then assist your child in locating the next blank page so he or she can write and illustrate his or her own story. Your child may dictate his or her account to you, or you may help your child sound out the words if he or she is not able to write independently. Encourage detailed illustrations with lots of color. Please use colored pencils or crayons and not markers. Our classroom expectation is to always have five or more colors on a finished assignment, so hold your child accountable to this requirement. Add labels to the illustration for additional writing practice, too.

This journal is, by far, the most requested in the class, so please return *The "Ouch" Book* in a day or two. Your child will then share his or her page in front of the class. Who knew "owies" could be so much fun?

Thanks for your help!

Sincerely,

_____

A Book About Our Scrapes, Bumps, Bruises, and Boo-Boos!

by

_____

Name: _____ Date: _____

Ouch! I Got Hurt!

Here's what happened . . .

_____

_____

_____

Dear Parents,

Your child has requested to take home *The Birthday Book*. This journal is an on-going collection of children's accounts of their long-awaited birthday fun. Please assist your child in writing and illustrating about his or her big day. The story might be centered around a favorite present, a special meal that was prepared, the delicious birthday cake and how it was decorated, relatives included in the celebration, a special birthday tradition you practice in your family, and so on.

> **Note:** *Please refrain from writing about a birthday party with school friends/peers. We make it a point not to discuss these events at school as hurt feelings sometimes arise. Thank you!*

Find the next empty page and instruct your child to write and illustrate about his or her birthday. Encourage five or more colors and lots of detail in the illustration. Please help your child write at least one sentence that corresponds to his or her picture. Make sure the text matches the illustration. You are welcome to sound out the words together, or your child can dictate to you. If capable, children are encouraged to write independently.

Return the journal in a couple of days so your child can read his or her page in front of the class. Questions, comments, and praise for their hard work will follow.

Thank you for your help!
Sincerely,

_____

The Birthday Book

by

_____

- -

_____

Name: _____ Date: _____

It was my birthday!

_____

_____

_____

_____

Dear Parents,

Getting new shoes is incredibly exciting! It is something that rarely goes unnoticed at school, too. "Look, _____ is wearing brand-new shoes today!" We see this fun event as another writing opportunity for kids. Children write enthusiastically about things that excite them (and things that actually happen to them). New shoes do just that! Your child might choose to write about your outing to the store, a special event that prompted the purchase, growing feet, and so on.

New shoes!

Find the next empty page and have your child illustrate the story of his or her new shoes. Next, help your child write a sentence or two about the experience. The writing can be done independently, or sentences can be sounded out together or dictated to you. Encourage best work with five or more colors and lots of detail in the drawing, as well as neat handwriting. The final product will be shared in front of the class. Children are always thrilled to show off their new shoes. Now this can take place in a written format, too.

Thank you for your help!

Sincerely,

_____

The New Shoes

A book about happy feet & excited kids!

by

Name: _____ Date: _____

I got new shoes!

_____

_____

_____

_____

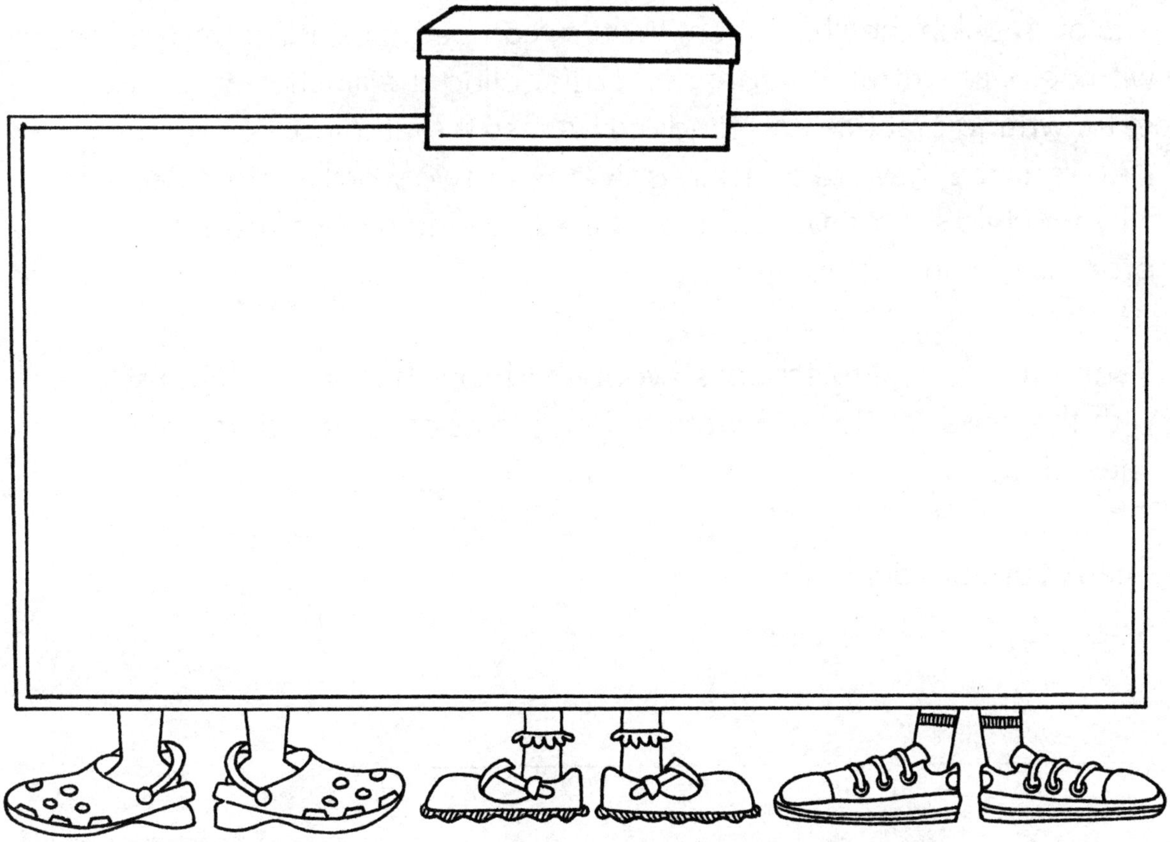

_____

Dear Parents,

Children love to share news about themselves, and a haircut is definitely newsworthy. In fact, a new haircut rarely goes unnoticed at school. Whether it's a new style or just a trim, we want to hear about the trip to the barbershop, salon, or wherever you get your hair done.

Have your child find the next empty page on the journal and illustrate and write about his or her haircut or hairdo. Prompt your child with questions, such as: *Why did you choose to get a haircut? Where did you go for it? What was your favorite part about getting a haircut? Can you think of any other interesting things that happened while you were getting your hair done?* Encourage neat handwriting, and five or more colors and lots of detail in the illustration. Writing can be dictated, sounded out with help, or written independently. Labeling the illustration provides extra writing practice and tends to be less threatening for emerging writers, since they are typically only one or two words long. Encourage all your child's attempts as he or she writes and always keep the process fun and celebratory.

Return the journal to school so your child can share his or her entry with the class. We look forward to hearing about every detail of the "new do."

Thank you for your help!
Sincerely,

_____

The "New Do"

by

Name: _____ Date: _____

I got a haircut!

_____

_____

_____

_____

_____

Dear Parents,

Your participation is requested in our "Traveling Tales" collaborative story. This journal is a progressive story that will circulate our class, giving every child an opportunity to add on to the story and contribute his or her great ideas. We are not sure where this story will end up, but it will be exciting to read as it grows from author to author throughout the year!

Upon receiving this journal, please begin by reading the completed entries to get a feel for the story to date. Next, generate possible ideas and extensions with your child. Have fun elaborating on the previous storyline. Your child may also decide it is time to introduce a new character or event. Be mindful to make sure your child's addition makes sense and extends the story in a non-confusing way.

On the next empty page in this journal, assist your child with his or her writing. Depending on your child's writing ability, any method of writing assistance is welcome. When illustrating the entry, ask your child to match the picture to the text and fill the page with color for a beautiful finished piece.

Thank you for your help with our shared story!

Sincerely,

_____

Traveling Tales

by

_____

- -

_____

Name: _____   Date: _____

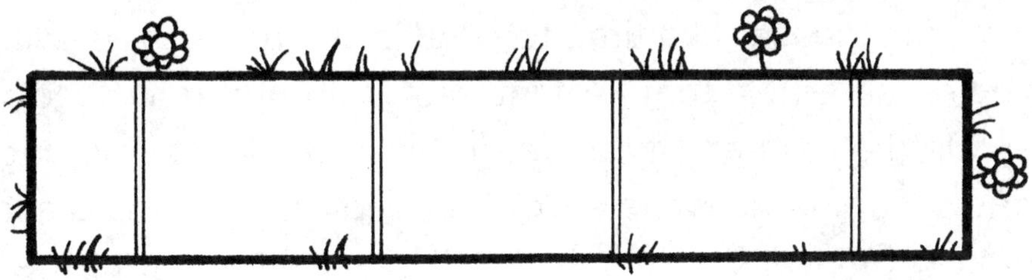

_____

_____

_____

_____

_____

Dear Parents,

In an effort to stay informed as a class, we have been referencing the newspaper to gather information. As more and more people receive their news online, we've specifically targeted the newspaper by navigating the index, various sections, and page numbers to find articles of interest. We have categorized news into world, national, local, sports, and business. When a timely article coincides with something we're studying, we make a point to read it directly from the newspaper.

To extend this practice, every student will have a turn as our weekly Class Reporter. Please take time to peruse the newspaper with your child and find an article that is of interest to him or her. Read the article together. On the next empty page of this journal, assist your child as he or she briefly summarizes the article. An illustration should accompany the summary. Cut out the selected article and attach it to the back of the page with tape or glue stick. On the smaller rectangle, have your child draw a self portrait from the neck up to indicate that he or she is the featured columnist for this article. Please return this journal next Monday so your child can share his or her entry with the class.

Thank you!
Sincerely,

_____

Class Reporter

by

_____

- -

_____

Name: _____   Date: _____

NEWS

☆ ☆

By: _____

Featured Columnist

_____

_____

_____

_____

Dear Parents,

This journal is about asking and answering all kinds of questions. Take time to read prior entries with your child so you can learn interesting facts and understand how you can participate on the next empty page. Our class is taking turns circulating this journal and posing questions to one another about anything. We're also familiarizing ourselves with question words, such as *who*, *what*, *where*, *why*, *when*, and *how*. Lastly, this journal provides practice for writing those tricky question marks.

Find the last completed page. The student that completed this entry has posed a question, and it's your child's assignment to search out the answer to it. Help your child search the Internet, encyclopedias, books, atlases, and other resources to find the answer. After discovering the answer, record it on your journal entry page. (Assist your child with writing as needed.) Then, it's your child's turn to generate a question for the next recipient of the journal. Questions can range in topic from sports to history, weather, geography, entertainment—anything goes! The bottom portion of the entry is designated for your new question. Encourage very neat writing as the next classmate will need to easily read it.

Instruct your child to take time tracing the dotted question marks on the page. Finally, read your child's question out loud, prompting your child to identify the "question word" in his or her question. Have your child underline that word.

As usual, thanks for your support!

Sincerely,

_____

The Question Journal

by

Name: _____ Date: _____

Dear Parents,

Pets definitely enrich our lives. These special members of the family have "tales" to share. From their quirky behavior to favorite pastimes, playful antics, and emotional milestones, your pets' news is newsworthy! Children request *The Pet Journal* as the need or desire arises. Maybe a pet has mastered a new trick, had babies, or got lost, or maybe something funny happened with your family pet. This journal provides a venue for any kind of pet-related story.

If your family doesn't have a pet, your child can write about a pet he or she adores outside your home—maybe a neighbor's or relative's pet. Your child is also welcome to write about a dream pet he or she wishes for but can't have for whatever reason. Encourage your child to get silly and creative, like wishing for an elephant if you live in an apartment.

Turn to the next empty page so your child can begin writing and illustrating his or her pet story. Depending on your child's writing abilities, assist him or her through dictation, sounding out words together, or copying words that you provide. Monitor and support your child if he or she is capable of writing independently. Like all good authors and illustrators, make sure your child's text matches his or her illustration. Encourage lots of color (at least five colors) and detail. We look forward to reading your child's real or fictional pet story.

Thanks for your help!
Sincerely,

_____

The Pet Journal

by

_____

- -

_____

Name: _____   Date: _____

All About My Pet!

_____

_____

_____

_____

Dear Parents,

This journal targets the math skill of measurement. Please assist your child in identifying three household items to measure and label. Help select items of varying dimensions so the measurements will be different and more challenging. On the next empty page of this journal, have your child illustrate each item and draw a dotted line indicating where the measurement was taken.

Each item will be measured with four different units of measurement. One will be a **standard** unit of measurement and the remaining three will be **nonstandard** units of your child's choosing (see below for possibilities).

Standard Units	Nonstandard Units
Inches	Pretzel sticks
Centimeters	Mini marshmallows
Feet	Pennies
Yard	Paper clips
Meter	Crayons

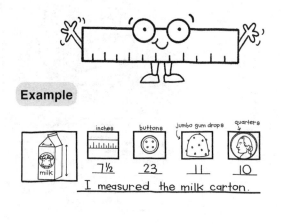

Example

As measurements are successfully taken, your child will record the measurements in the appropriate spaces. Take time to demonstrate how to measure the perimeter of an object if an item is round or stuffed. Wrap string or ribbon around the perimeter, mark it, then lay it flat to measure.

Thanks for your help. Happy measuring!

Sincerely,

_____

Measurement Math Journal

by

_____

- - - - - - - - - - - - - - - - -

_____

Name: _____ Date: _____

Dear Parents,

This math-related journal reinforces counting, one-to-one correspondence, addition, and number-writing practice through the use of number cubes.

With your child, roll the three enclosed number cubes. Replicate the numbers rolled on each cube by drawing the same number of dots on the indicated squares. Record the numbers on the corresponding lines below the squares. Next, have your child count all the dots to get a total. Record the total number to complete a number sentence (record the total twice—in the box and on the line below). If number recall is a challenge, write out the number on a separate piece of paper so your child can copy it, or write the number in dots for your child to trace.

Using the total number, your child must search throughout your home to identify and count the same number of a household object. For instance, if your total is 11, your child might walk around the house and count eleven windows or cups or ping-pong balls . . . you decide. Have your child write a brief sentence stating what was found along with the math sentence. For example, "I counted 8 oranges in my house." In the empty space, instruct your child to draw pictures of the objects matching the totals.

Thanks for your help. Happy counting!
Sincerely,

_____

Number Cubes

Math Journal

by

_____

- -

_____

Name: _____ Date: _____

☐ + ☐ + ☐ = ☐

___   ___   ___   ___

_____

☐ + ☐ + ☐ = ☐

___   ___   ___   ___

_____

Individual Shape Books

The following seven titles are a collection of individual shape books. The books' shapes reinforce the writing topics and allow for artistic opportunities. Each child creates a four- or five-page book, completed entirely in the classroom. Publishing a book may take a full week or more, but these finished projects offer academic depth and make adorable keepsakes.

Each shape book comes with directions for classroom implementation and a description of the assignment. All shape books come with template pages for student writing. Feel free to modify the lines to better suit your student population, giving children a format that will ultimately lead to a successful writing piece.

While writing is the primary focus in these books, art is also an important component. Value the artwork as much as the writing. The artistic element provides practice in following directions, an opportunity for creative license, and an enjoyable outlet that occupies children as you assist others with writing. The illustrations should complement the writing and, consequently, the illustrating process should be given equal emphasis with consistent expectations.

Consider making custom rubrics for the shape books. (A sample rubric is provided for The "Ch" Book.) The time and hard work required to make these books warrants an official rubric. Determine which criteria you value most and create a rubric to accompany each title. Completed shape books are timely writing samples that document student growth. Parents will love them because they are adorable keepsakes. These books may be somewhat time-consuming to produce but well worth the effort.

Titles include:

1. **The Barn Book** – Children write and illustrate a fiction or nonfiction book about farm life.

2. **The "Ch" Book** – Focusing on the digraph "ch," children illustrate and label "ch" words on each page of their book.

3. **The "Sh" Book** – Not to be outdone by The "Ch" Book, "sh" words will have their time in the spotlight as children illustrate and label them.

4. **The Bug-Expert Book** – Children write fiction or nonfiction insect stories.

5. **The Deep-Sea Submarine Book** – Following a pretend dive to the depths of the ocean, children write about and illustrate their journey.

6. **The Suitcase Book** – Packing a suitcase for a specific destination, children write and illustrate the contents of their luggage and why it was necessary to pack them.

7. **My Dream Lunch Book** – Children write and illustrate their dream lunch to pack for school.

Individual Shape Book: The Barn Book

Use this barn shape book for a fiction or nonfiction writing assignment. It's a perfect complement to your farm unit or can be a fun, fictional writing assignment set in a farm.

Farm-animal clip art is included below. The simplistic illustrations are designed to help children successfully copy or draw their own animals. Illustrated animals can also double as laminated puppets that walk through the finished story. Instruct children to draw, color, and cut out a farm animal. Laminate each animal and punch a small hole on it. Tie a string through the hole and attach it to a 10- to 12-inch string hanging from a hole punched at the top of the barn cover (page 53). Manipulating the animal puppets through the pages is absolute fun!

Be sure to cut inside the dotted lines surrounding the barn, leaving a margin of white that borders the perimeter of the barn and corresponding writing pages. Have children print the title on the top portion of the barn door and their name on the line at the bottom of the door.

Make three or four copies of the interior template (page 54) for each child. Attach the pages to the cover with staples on the side. Have children draw in the blank space at the top of the page. Lines are provided for writing, but feel free to make adaptations to accommodate your children. Assist children in their writing attempts and encourage them to share their completed stories.

Animal Clip Art

Individual Shape Book: The "Ch" Book

This chocolate-chip shape book targets the "ch" digraph and helps children discriminate its sound. Before handing out the book templates to children, brainstorm as many "ch" words as possible with the class and record them on chart paper. Refer to a dictionary to expand your list, if needed. As you read the list, exaggerate the /ch/ sound to help children master it.

Consider introducing this book in time for Valentine's Day, when children have chocolate treats on their mind. February also seems to be that magical time of the school year when kindergartners gain writing confidence and their independent writing skills start to take off. Use this book to assess how capably they can write without assistance. (The provided rubric states this as an expectation.) Kindergartners might label their drawing by simply writing a word; first and second graders can write their "ch" words in the context of completed sentences. Modify the lines provided so adequate space is available. Children should complete 4 to 6 pages over the course of a week. (Be certain to hide the word list you generated.) The completed book serves as timely documentation for spring parent/teacher conferences.

For the book cover, trace the provided chocolate-chip outline (page 56) onto oak tag or photocopy on card stock. Cut out the chocolate-chip shape and cover with aluminum foil, helping young children tape edges down on the back. Use a black permanent marker to write *The "Ch" Book* on the foil cover and draw a line for the student's name.

Make four to six photocopies of the interior page (page 57) for each child. Cut out the pages, leaving a margin of white around the perimeter. Have children illustrate one "ch" word per page, and then write that word without help. (Some clip art is included on page 56.) Illustrations should fill a generous portion of the page. Encourage children to use five or more colors on their drawings.

Photocopy the chocolate-chip rubric (page 58) on card stock and display as the back cover. Assemble the books with a single staple at the top of the chocolate chip. Once books are completed and assembled, return them to children and instruct them to self-assess their work based on the four criteria. Children will rate their work by drawing a smiley, straight, or sad face in the circles. Celebrate these festive books with a sampling of chocolate kisses!

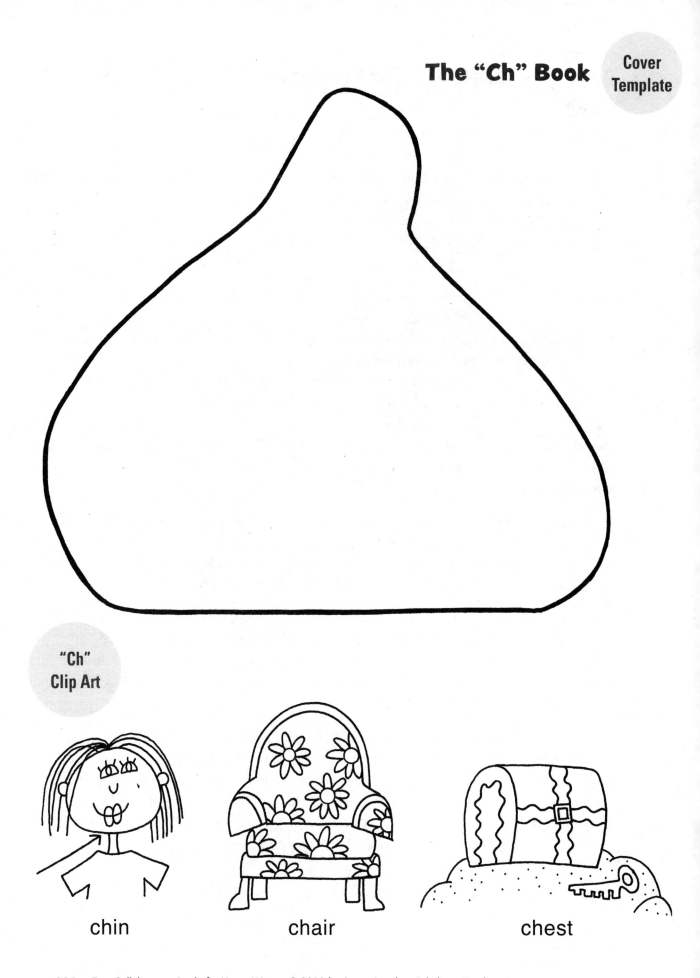

"Ch" Clip Art

chin   chair   chest

The "Ch" Book

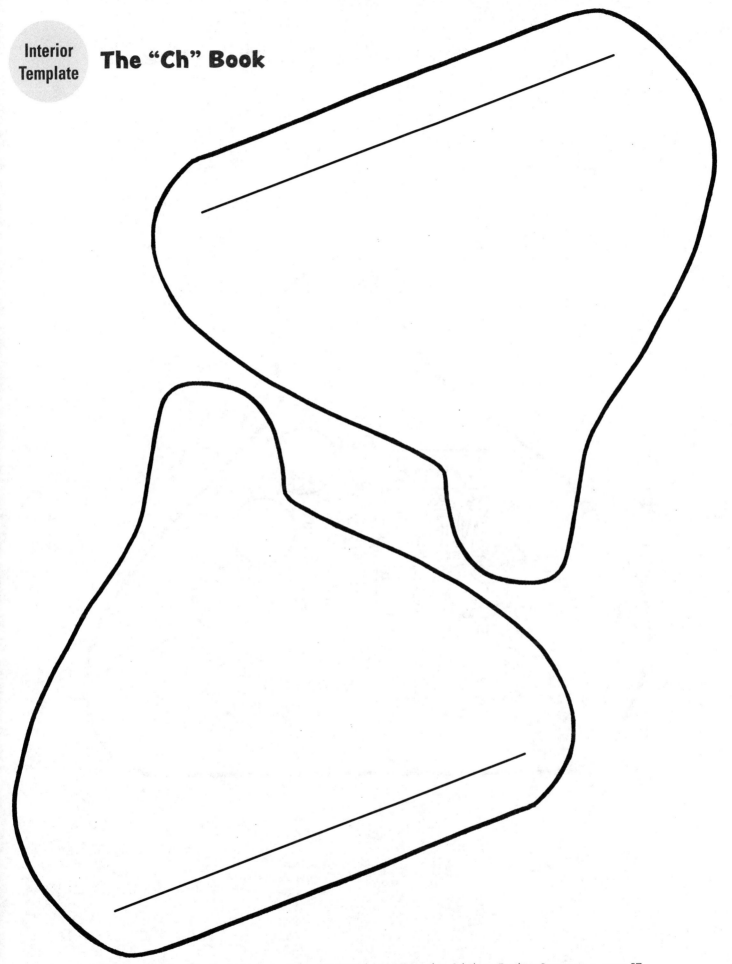

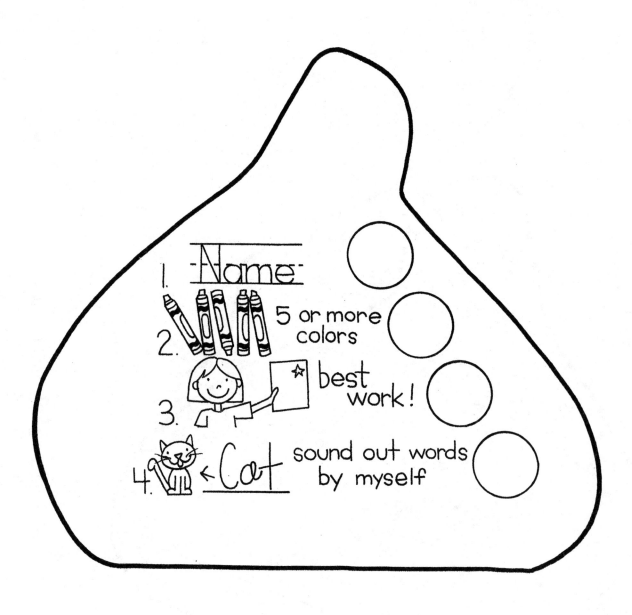

1. Name _____

2. 5 or more colors

3. best work!

4. Cat ← sound out words by myself

The *"Sh" Book* helps children become more comfortable in identifying the "sh" digraph and its corresponding sound. In preparation for this assignment, invite children to generate as many "sh" words as they can and record these on chart paper. If necessary, refer to the dictionary to finalize your list. Inform children that they will encounter this sound often and that its sound will become very recognizable. Use the universal "Shhhh/quiet" gesture (index finger to pursed lips) to accompany the sound. Remind students that while this digraph or sound can be found anywhere in a given word, this assignment exclusively involves words beginning with the "sh" sound.

Photocopy the shirt cover (page 60) on card stock to give it more durability and consider laminating once it's decorated. You can challenge children to replicate the shirt they're actually wearing that day or design a shirt pattern/logo of their own. The tag at the back of the T-shirt is designated for the student's name. Any art medium will work!

Students' books can be four to six pages long, with each page highlighting a different "sh" word. As with *The "Ch" Book*, make the labeling and/or writing an expectation. At the kindergarten level, this one-word label should be achievable since the first two letters of the word are already provided. Challenge children to stretch out the remainder of their word and record what they hear. Older students with more writing experience should attempt a sentence or two per page, elaborating on the "sh" word. For example: *The sheriff caught three bad outlaws who robbed a bank.* Modify the provided writing lines to expand their writing space, if needed. Illustrations should be generously sized with adequate detail and five or more colors.

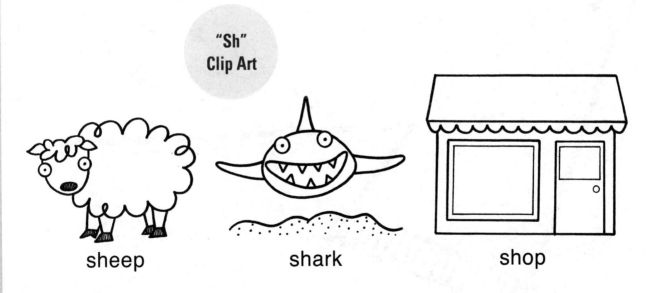

"Sh" Clip Art

sheep   shark   shop

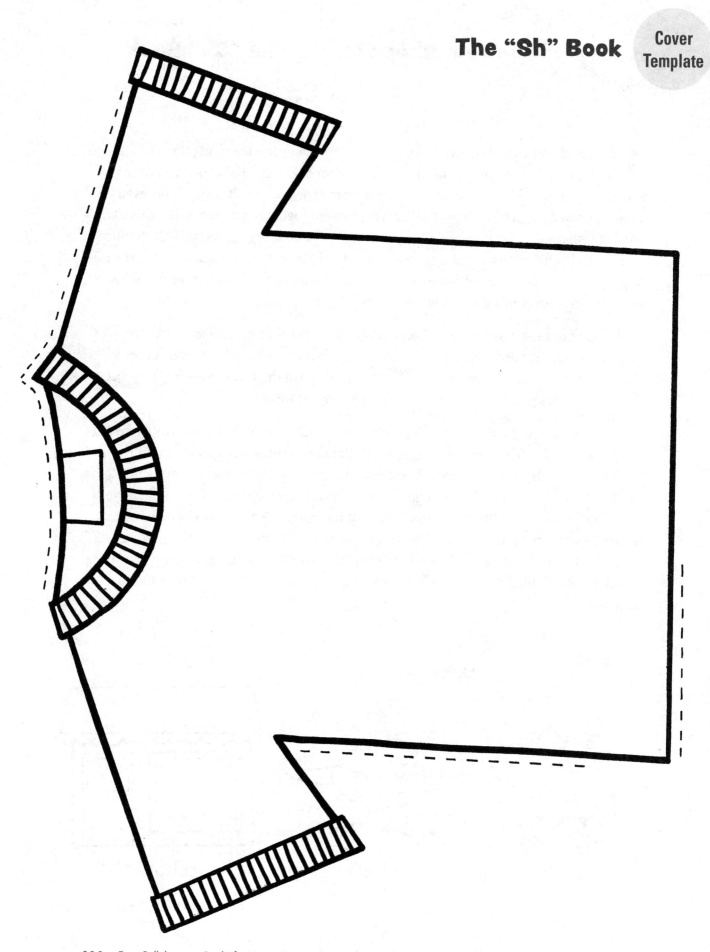

25 Best-Ever Collaborative Books for Young Writers © 2012 by Susan Stroeher, Scholastic Teaching Resources • page 60

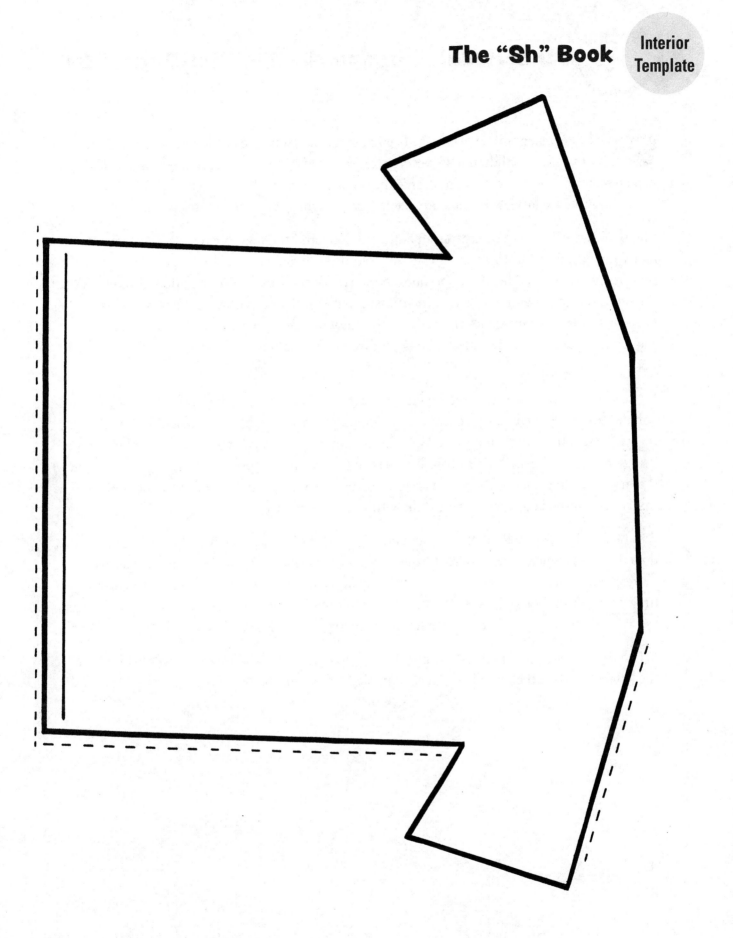

Shaped like a magnifying glass, *The Bug-Expert Book* can be the culminating project in an insect unit, after children have become "experts" on common insects, their basic traits, habits, habitats, and more. Children can either create a fictional bug story or recap insect facts. They can write exclusively about a favorite insect or highlight a different insect on each page.

The book's transparent cover gives an authentic look and the magnified central insect adds an extra-special touch. Instruct children to color their magnifying glass (page 62) and write their name on the handle. Then cut out the interior of the glass (inside the dotted line) and the outer perimeter and laminate. (The transparent lamination will resemble a real magnifying glass.) Use the same image for the back cover, but white out the interior dotted lines and leave the inside intact. Write the title of the book directly on the transparent laminate with a black permanent marker.

Invite children to choose an insect to illustrate for their book cover. Appropriate sizing will enhance the magnified look so encourage children to generously fill the provided rectangle with their illustration. Have them use a lot of color with heavy coverage for on their insect. Consider using only colored pencils as crayons can melt in the lamination process. Help children cut out the insect, leaving a margin of white around the perimeter. Laminate the illustration and tape the insect behind the laminated cover to "show through the glass."

For the interior (page 64), photocopy and cut out three or four pages per child. Cut inside the dotted line, leaving a thin margin of white around the perimeter of the magnifying glass and corresponding writing pages. Provide insect clip art (page 90) for children to reference as they draw their illustrations. Allow up to a week for children to complete their books. For best results, assign one page a day and emphasize hard work. Encourage illustrations to match text.

When their books are completed, help children staple the cover and interior pages together on the extended tab at the top. These finished books will be "all the BUZZ"!

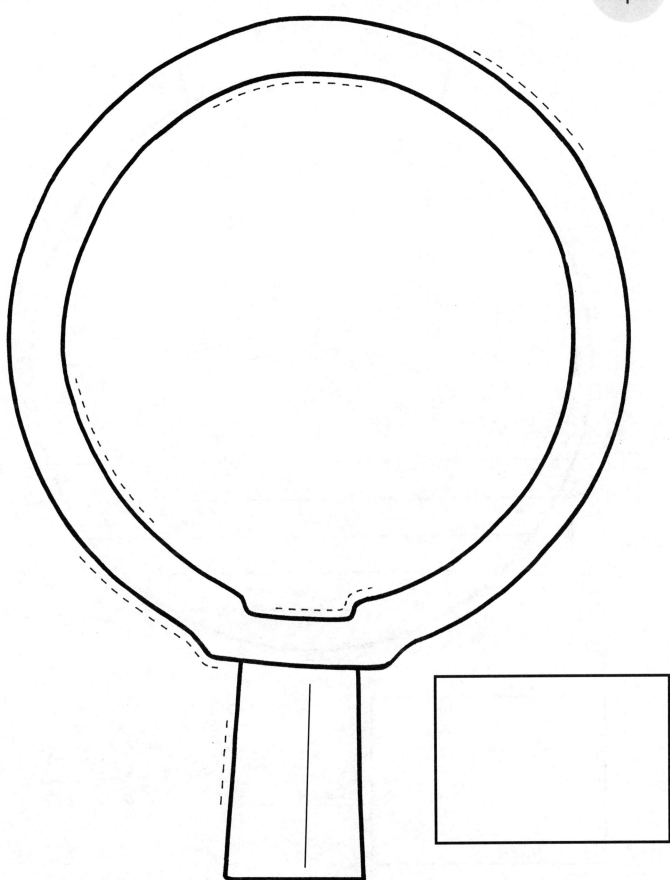

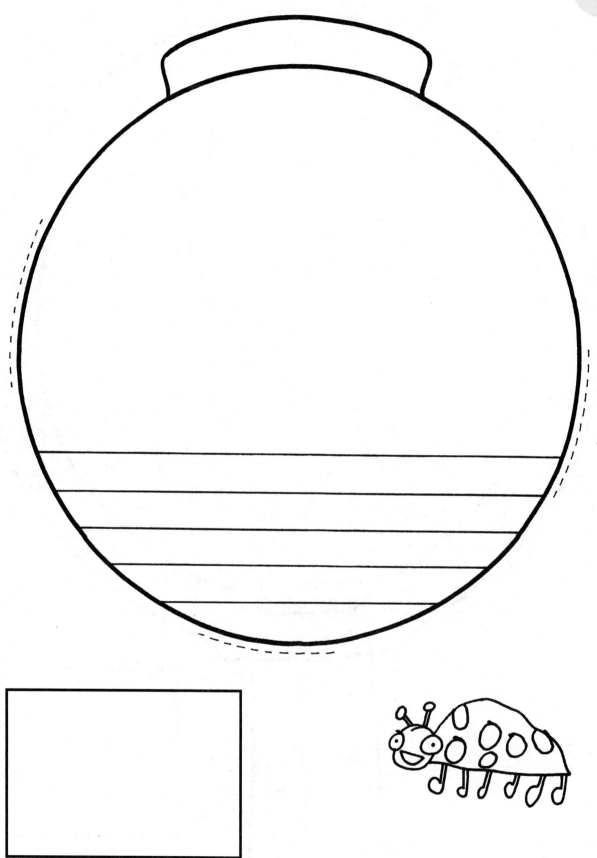

The Bug-Expert Book

With this book, children pretend to dive into the ocean depths with personal deep-sea submarines. Invite them to use this template to create a:

• simple counting book, in which readers count different ocean life on each page.

• nonfiction book with ocean-animal facts.

• fiction story involving a submarine adventure.

For the cover (page 66), instruct children to write their name on the line provided. Then have them draw a self-portrait (from the waist up) in the central window of the submarine to show themselves diving deep to observe all the underwater wonders. On the four windows at the top of the sub, have children draw special family members, such as parents, siblings, or pets, who join in their deep-sea adventure. Encourage them to draw with colored pencils, making clear that you expect detailed illustrations and adequate color with heavy coverage. The submarine can be colored using watercolors or pencils. (Avoid crayons as they will likely melt in the lamination process.) Cut out the submarine and laminate.

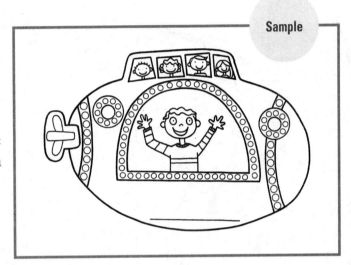

Sample

Photocopy three to four blank interior pages (page 67) for every child. Modify the lines for specific student needs and assist children with writing, as necessary. Staple all completed pages together at the top of the submarine. A cover sample is provided above.

* If you choose to have children create counting books, cut and paste the lines below onto each interior page. Children should write a number on the small line and use the longer line to identify the ocean animal. For example, "I saw 5 crabs." Number writing and labeling should be the focus of this assignment.

I saw ____ _____.

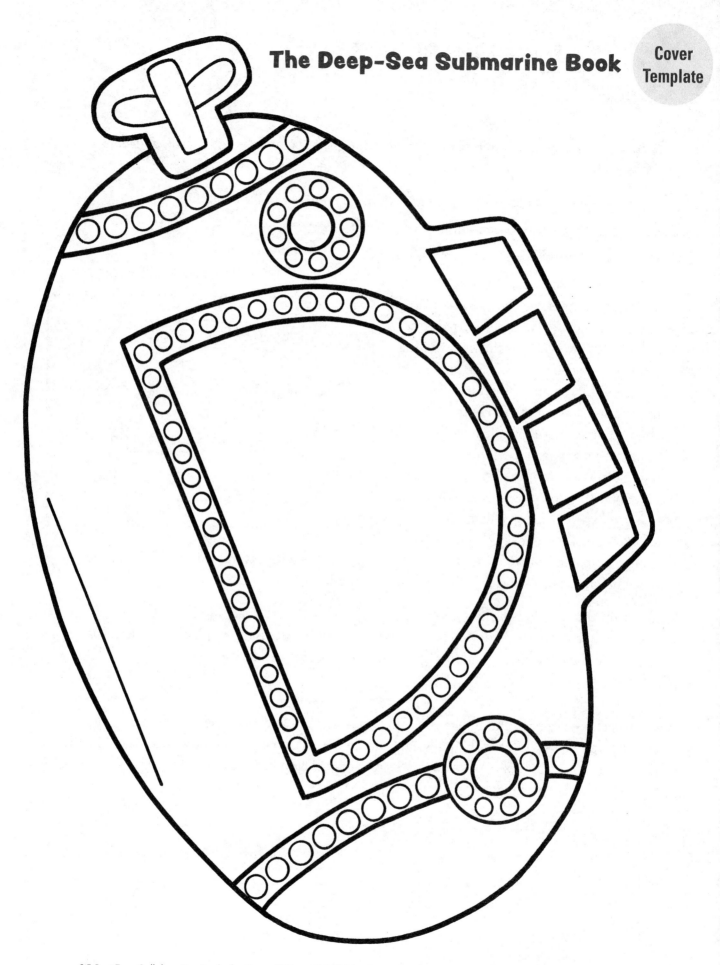

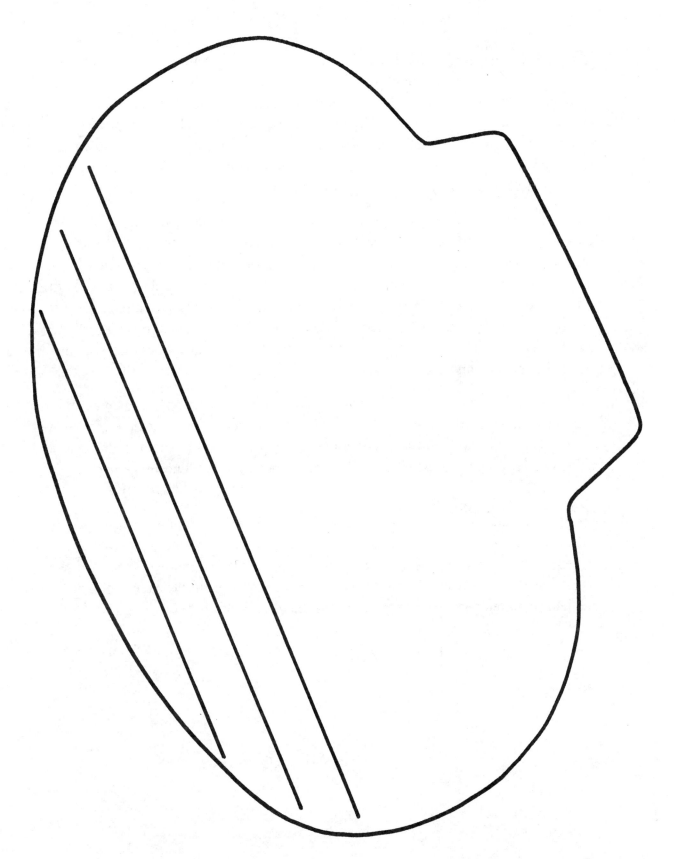

In this fun, motivating writing assignment, each child creates his or her own suitcase book, packs its contents, and writes about two or three specific items, detailing why it was important to pack them. Travel locations will determine what will be appropriate and/or necessary to pack. Allow children to choose an actual travel destination or a fictional one, or specify a location related to a current unit of study. Travel destinations can include cities; countries; continents; landmarks; specific regions, such as the jungle, desert, or ocean; the moon; or fictional places, like a fairytale setting.

Decorating the book cover (page 69) can be an art project in itself. Encourage children to color, paint, or decoupage their piece of luggage to show their individual tastes and interests. If possible, provide several finished examples so children can get a sense of your art expectations and begin to brainstorm their own ideas. Insist on quality work with five or more colors and heavy coverage. Have children work in pencil to sketch their designs and, upon your approval, outline their pictures with a black permanent marker. Children may then color them with colored pencils or paints. Use a permanent marker to outline the title and student's name, then laminate the front covers.

The first interior template (page 70) will display the contents of the suitcase. Invite children to think about where they are traveling and how the location's climate, features, landmarks, native population, and so on, will determine what they pack. Children must illustrate six to eight items on this page and label each with one or two words. Encourage amazing detail and color.

For the remainder of the book, make two or three copies of the writing template (page 71) for each child. On each page, children will highlight a particular item in the suitcase and explain why or how it was used in their imaginary travels. Have children draw themselves actually using the item and write text to match. Once completed, staple the pages together and hang children's books on a wall from their handles. Have fun!

The Suitcase Book

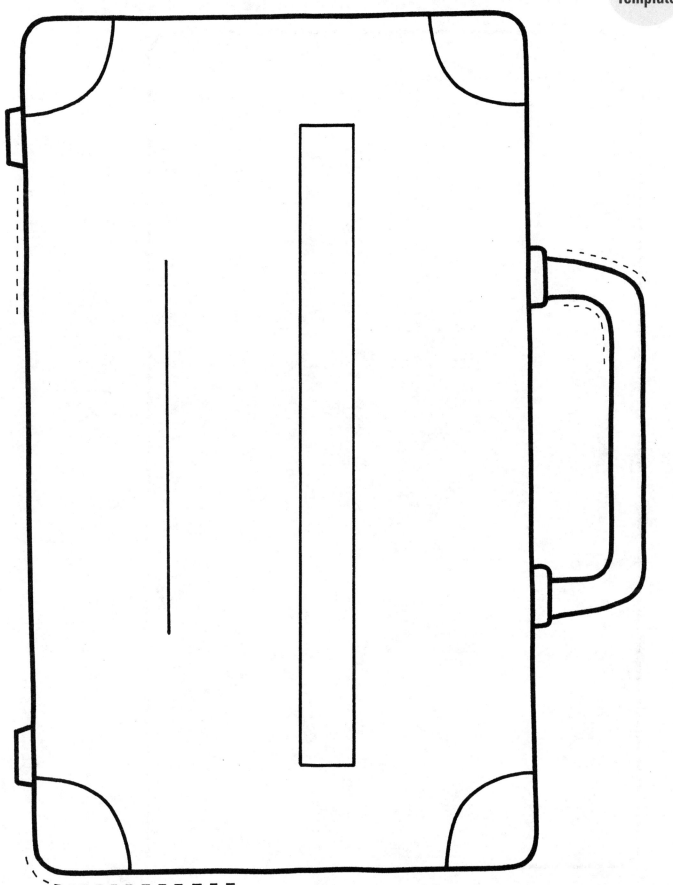

The Suitcase Book

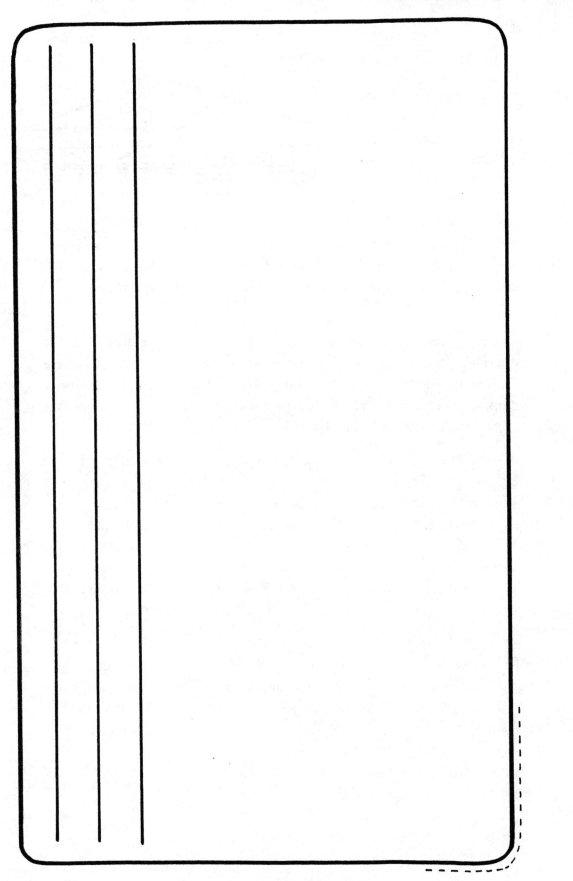

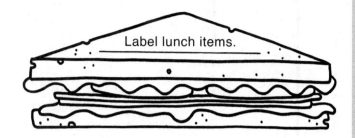

Label lunch items.

Packing lunch can turn into a routine rut—same old meal with little variety. Children will enjoy packing their dream lunch in this deliciously motivating shape book. Each child will personalize his or her own lunch bag and pack four lunch items that represent a healthy variety. Lunch items will be illustrated, colored, cut out, and laminated, and children will write about them on the following pages. In addition to a labeled fork, spoon, and napkin that accompany the food, children can also write themselves a lunch note, pretending to be Mom or Dad (page 75).

For the lunch-bag covers (page 73), encourage children to illustrate an object that represents their interests (for example, baseball, heart, insect, or puppy) and repeat it across the bag. Have children first sketch with pencil and then, upon your approval, outline their drawings with a black permanent marker. Provide them with colored pencils or watercolors to add color. Laminate the covers when completed.

Spend time discussing what a typical packed lunch looks like, encouraging children to embellish to make the lunch choices extra special. Emphasize healthy selections that represent four different food groups—fruits, vegetables, grain, and protein. Provide children with paper and pencil to illustrate their food choices. You may want to draw a circle or square to ensure correct sizing. Once you approve their sketches, have them outline their drawings with a permanent black marker and color them with colored pencils. Help them cut out their foods, making sure to leave a margin of white around the drawings. Laminate for durability. Create a pocket on the inside of the front cover to house the food items, utensils, and lunch note.

Make three or four copies of the writing template (page 74) for each child. Invite children to use each page to detail a portion of their lunch. Children can talk about what food group it represents or write about personal food preferences. For example, "I packed key lime yogurt with real strawberries for dessert!" or "Turkey is from the protein group. I have a turkey sandwich." or "I love to dip carrot sticks in Ranch dressing. Carrots are vegetables." When completed, staple the pages together and cut out the inside of the bag handle so bags can be hung on thumbtacks.

My Dream Lunch Book

Cover
Template

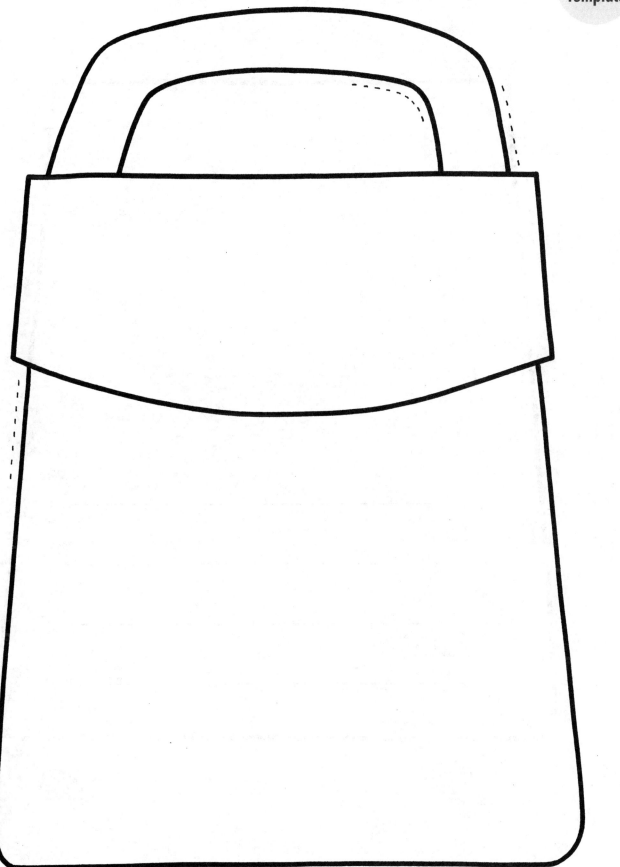

My Dream Lunch Book

Collaborative Class Books

Class books involve children creating and completing individual pages to contribute to a collaborative book centered around a common theme or writing prompt. These writing assignments can be completed in a day, but may take as many as three days, depending on the topic's complexity.

Class books require you to create a front and back cover to house children's pages. Children will complete their own pages during class time. Your student population and the time of year will dictate how extensively children will write. Always modify the writing space with lines, spaces, dotted lines, sentence starters, and so on, to best support your students.

Beyond writing, these six class books incorporate simple artistic components that add to their appeal. A description of the book, art suggestions, logistical sequence, and page templates are included, where applicable, for easy class execution.

When a book has been completed and bound, put it on permanent display at your classroom library and send a "press release" home, announcing the class's latest publication. Allow children to check out the book. At the end of the year, dismantle all books so individual pages can be sent home with their respective authors.

Titles include:

1. The Zoo Book – Children write about and illustrate a pretend sleepover with a zoo animal of their choosing.

2. "Please Pass the Sugar, Mr. President" – Invite children to celebrate Presidents' Day by writing about and illustrating an imaginary tea party where President Washington or Lincoln is invited. Be sure to build children's background knowledge about these important American figures before giving this writing assignment.

3. "Pizza, Please" – This fun book is housed in a small pizza box. Children write about what kind of pizza they would order if they were a particular animal or character. Fun fiction!

4. Bed Bugs – Children imagine crawling into bed and discovering an overnight bug guest. Relying on their prior knowledge about insects, children can embellish on real facts or recount factual information.

5. Magical Mail – Children will enjoy writing to their favorite fairytale character to ask a question pertaining to his or her classic story.

6. Class Comics – What can be more fun than creating your own comic book? Children will enjoy drawing characters, writing dialogues, and sharing their comics with the class.

Invite children to imagine spending the night at the zoo with an animal of their choice right in its cage! What animal will they choose? What fun/mischief/adventure will they share together?

Spend time brainstorming animals and, when applicable, comment on diet, behaviors, attributes, and other factual information about the animals to enhance children's stories. Based on facts already known about the animals, children can pretend to partake in behaviors the animals naturally display or just recount regular sleepover fun. For instance, knowing that monkeys eat bananas, a child might write: *After swinging in the monkey cage, we were thirsty, so we drank one banana milkshake after the next!*

Instruct children to create their wonderful stories on their individual writing template (page 79). They can dictate their ideas to an adult, sound out words with help, or write on their own. Encourage children to illustrate themselves in the cage with their selected animal. Spend a few minutes to demonstrate the desired sizing of the illustrations. Pajamas are the appropriate attire for this assignment, so encourage children to add detail to their jammies, like the kids on the front cover (page 78). It might be fun to assign pajama patterns to match or reference their animal in some way; for example, bananas sprinkled across the pajama top and bottoms would be ideal for a visit with a monkey. Remind children that their writing and illustration should support each other. As usual, request that children use colored pencils and strive for at least five or more colors.

The final step is to add the bars of the cage. In advance, cut skinny strips of black construction paper (approximately 1/8-inch thick). Demonstrate how to mark off seven equal increments across their cage using a ruler. Have children glide a glue stick across the strips of paper and position them vertically on their cage to make the setting look more authentic!

Have fun with this imaginative writing assignment. Whether it's with the "king of the beasts," a wet seal, or the cutest baby penguin, your class will enjoy creating this fictional writing piece.

The Zoo Book

by

_____

- -

_____

Name: _____ Date: _____

_____

_____

_____

_____

For Presidents' Day, present children with this opportunity to write historical fiction by having them invite either George Washington or Abraham Lincoln to a tea party! Children will write about a question they ask their president of choice based on facts they already know about their guest. Children will also color and write a tea-party invitation to attach to their page.

Preface the assignment by reading nonfiction books about both presidents so children gain information about their potential guest. Spend a week or more reading in anticipation of Presidents' Day. As interesting facts emerge, record them on chart paper so children can refer to them once the activity is underway.

Have children decide which president they will invite and write out their invitation (page 83). They should write the president's name on the top line and state the invitation on the bottom lines ("Please come to my tea party" or some variation). Use a string to suspend the tea bag from the teacup, and instruct children to write "From: (their name)" on the tea bag (page 83). Color and decorate the teacup as well. Punch holes on the circular markings and tape or glue finished invitations to the writing template (page 82).

Assist children in writing about the pretend conversation they had over tea, making sure they include some factual information. For example: "If President Lincoln had tea with me, I would ask him what was the farthest distance he ever walked to borrow a book," or "What kind of important papers do you store in your tall top hat?"

Have children illustrate and color a picture of themselves with President Lincoln or Washington, sitting on a stool or at the center of the table. Easy step-by-step directions for how to draw either president can be found on page 83. Instruct children to draw cupcakes, fruit, scones, cookies, and other goodies on the empty tiered plate. All coloring should be done with colored pencils.

"Please Pass the Sugar, Mr. President"

by

_____

- -

_____

Name: _____   Date: _____

Tape invitation here

_____

_____

_____

_____

_____

_____

Invitation

Tea bag

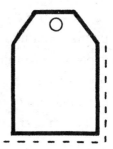

Draw President Abraham Lincoln

Draw President George Washington

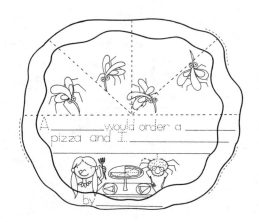

Children will love this imaginative, silly opportunity for fictional writing! If possible, get a small pizza box (10 to 12 inches) from your local pizzeria to serve as a unique cover for this particular class book.

To create the cover, flip the pizza box inside out so the outside is blank. Color and cut out the "Pizza, Please!" front cover (page 85), laminate, and tape to the center of the pizza box. Students' pizza page entries can be stored as loose, individual pieces or compiled in a book format with holes punched at the top or side and secured with small metal rings. Preface the assignment by taking a survey of children's personal pizza preferences. Collect the data and create a class graph. Then present the class with the small pizza box to introduce the latest class book, *"Pizza, Please!"*

Review children's popular pizza selections, then pose the question: *"Now what kind of pizza do you suppose a cow would order?"* Generate additional ideas with the class by brainstorming animals, cartoon characters, fairytale characters, aliens, monsters, and more. Reverse the question by asking, *"If I have a pizza with toothpaste on it, who do you think ordered it?"* (maybe a dentist or the Tooth Fairy) Have fun with this discussion and send children off to their desks with plenty of ideas.

Invite children to write about and illustrate their fictional pizza on individual pizza templates (page 86). A sentence starter is already provided, but feel free to omit or alter the sentence for your own needs. Proficient writers can extend their stories on the back of their page.

Have children decorate the top half of the pizza (dotted into slices) with the preferred topping of their chosen animal, character, or monster. For example, it makes sense that a spider would order a pizza with extra mosquitoes. Instruct children to color and decorate the pizza as well. Model a slightly brown crust and orange cheesy topping with red sauce. Children can fill in the empty space directly below the writing with a picture of themselves dining (or not) with their pizza "date." Remind children to color their page with five or more colors. Then cut out the individual pizzas and store them in the pizza box. Encourage children to replicate the class graph on the back of their pizza with tally marks. Allow students to take turns checking out the pizza-box book so families can enjoy and, of course, order pizza for dinner!

"Pizza, Please!"

by

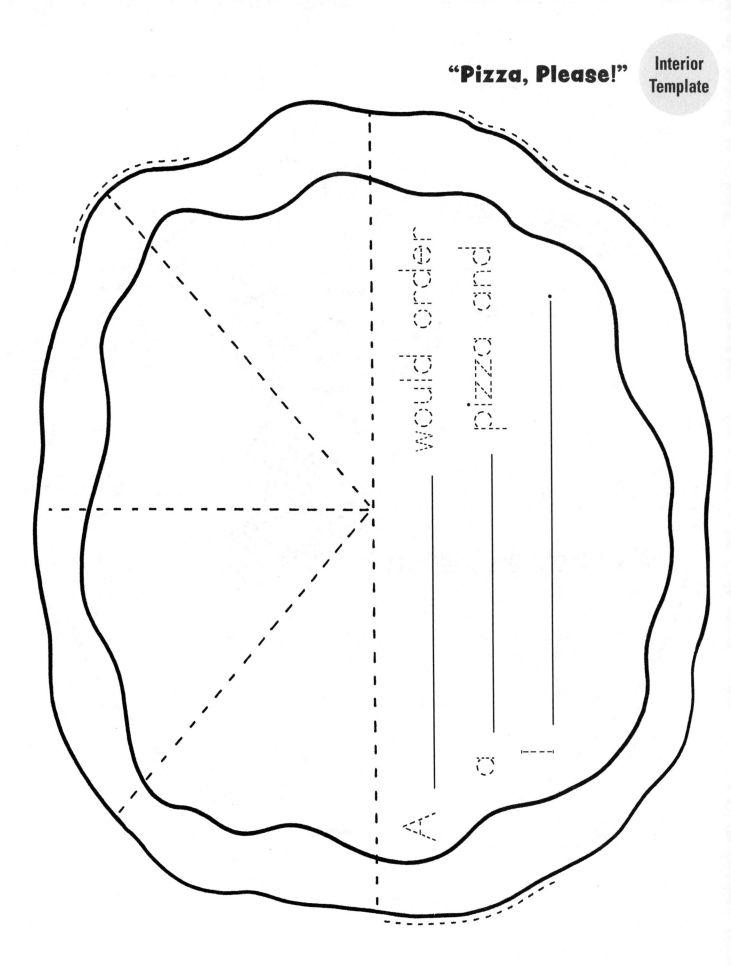

Would order

pizza and

A

C

I

Bed Bugs is a fun, imaginative writing assignment in which children pretend to discover a bug under their covers! On the writing template (page 89), children write the type of insect they found, then relay a fact about their insect or elaborate on their sleepover adventures. Provide insect facts for children to copy or restate. If needed, assist them with their writing by either sounding out words together, writing out words for them to copy, or scribing for the child as he or she dictates. Feel free to modify the writing lines provided to better serve your student population.

In addition to the writing component, this activity has several art requirements. To start, have children draw their insect in the center of the dotted rectangle on the writing page. For children's reference, consider enlarging the critter clip art (page 90) on chart paper or simply distribute photocopies. Next, invite children to draw a self-portrait from the neck up on the pillow and color the bed frame. Finally, on the box provided on page 90, have them design and decorate a quilt in a plaid, harlequin, or mixed pattern (see right). Take time to demonstrate the three options, using a ruler to segment the quilt into a consistent pattern. Have children work in pencil initially and, upon your approval, outline their pattern with a black permanent marker. Demonstrate how to draw dashes to represent stitches on a quilt.

Encourage children to use crayons or colored pencils on their quilts to achieve a broader range of color. The goal is to create a quilt bursting with color. Require five or more colors and have children color heavily so the quilt really pops. The finished quilts definitely add to the books' appeal, as each one is unique with its own color combinations and intricate designs. When finished, help children cut out and staple the completed quilt on top of the bug on their writing page so it can be lifted to reveal the surprise critter. Display the completed pages on a wall or compile them to create a class book.

ladybug

Quilt Patterns

Plaid Design: Follow these step-by-step instructions for drawing the plaid motif.

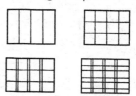

Harlequin Design: When outlining in black, students might consider broken black lines or dashes to resemble stitching.

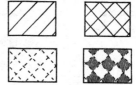

Mixed Pattern Design: Once the quilt is equally segmented, alternate squares with striped, dotted, and decorated designs.

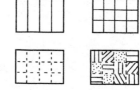

Bed Bugs

by

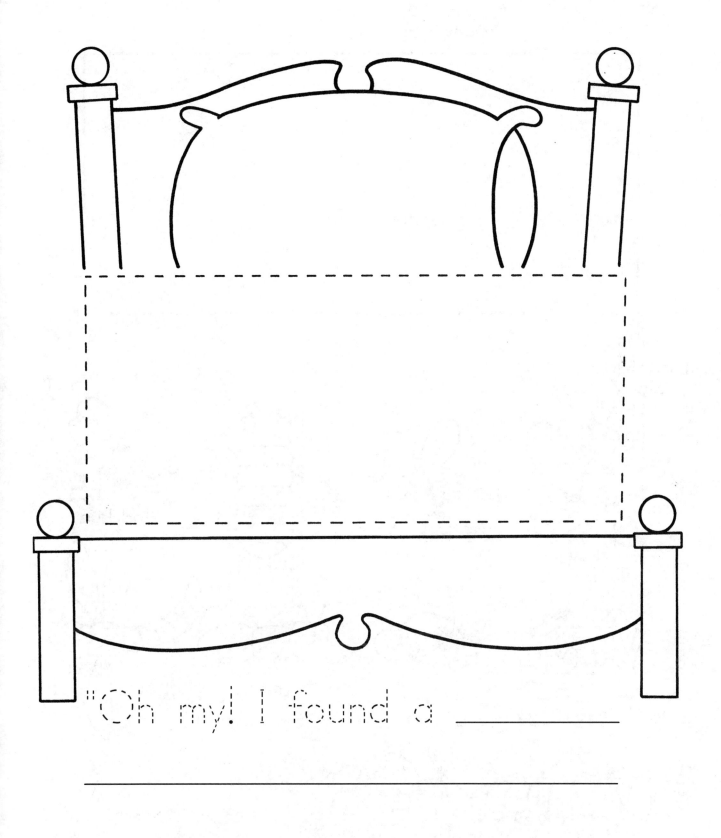

"Oh my! I found a _____

_____

_____.

Name: _____ Date: _____

Draw your quilt pattern here:

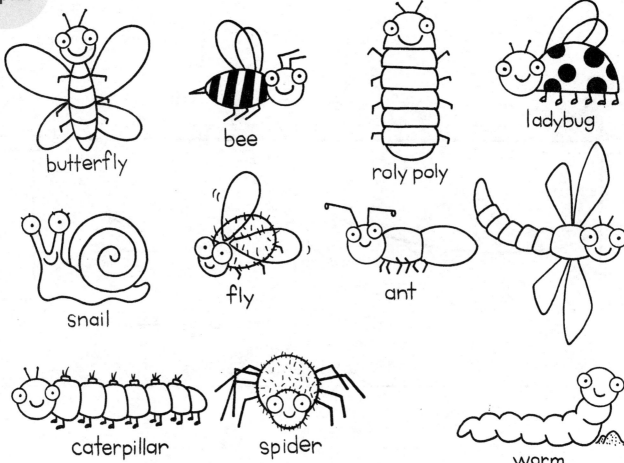

Insect
Clip Art

butterfly

bee

roly poly

ladybug

snail

fly

ant

caterpillar

spider

worm

Children will love this assignment in which they write to a favorite fairytale character. To prepare for this assignment, spend a few weeks reading multiple versions of classic fairytales and familiarize children with the characters. Multiple versions allow for comparing and contrasting, and children can identify similarities and differences among the stories. As a culminating project, every child will write a postcard to his or her favorite character and pose a question pertaining to the story and/or character. Assist children in generating a question and writing it on the postcard (page 93). In addition, have children draw a picture of themselves and the character. To further motivate children, tell them that the collection of postcards will be "magically" delivered to Fairytale Land and distributed to the appropriate characters. In the days that follow, make sure each child receives a return postcard with a response written by the character. Compile the postcards to create a class book titled, *Magical Mail*.

Below is a list of fairytales and their corresponding main characters:

"Goldilocks and the Three Bears" — Goldilocks, Papa Bear, Mama Bear, and Baby Bear

"The Three Little Pigs" — First Pig (straw), Second Pig (sticks), Third Pig (bricks), and Big Bad Wolf

"The Gingerbread Man" — Gingerbread Man, Old Woman/Old Man, and Fox

"Jack and the Beanstalk" — Jack, The Giant, and the Goose

"Three Billy Goats Gruff" — Smallest Billy Goat, Middle Billy Goat, Largest Billy Goat, and Mean Troll

"Little Red Riding Hood" — Little Red Riding Hood, Granny, Wolf

Magical Mail

by

_____

- -

_____

Name: _____   Date: _____

Collaborative Class Book: Class Comics

A pig met a new friend.   They played a game of catch.   They shared a vanilla milkshake.

A class comic book offers a fun writing venue for kids. For this class book, children will create their own comic strip complete with dialogue and narration. Prior to this assignment, start collecting the comic pages from the Sunday papers. Search out comics that are amusing, age-appropriate, and easily understood by your student population. Display several examples and point out what the different comic strips have in common; for example, the speech bubbles, the frames of the comic strip, on-going dialogue between characters and, sometimes, a written narrative below the strip. Show your students the difference between the Sunday funnies and those found in the daily newspaper. Notice how size and color add to the reading enjoyment. Next, introduce the front cover of the soon-to-be *Class Comics*.

To make the front cover, decoupage the cover template (page 95) with individual frames from the colorful Sunday comic pages, surrounding the title strip in the center. Laminate once the paper is completely dry.

Photocopy the writing template with speech bubbles (page 96) for each child. Encourage children to draw and write about people, animals, aliens, monsters, themselves, anything! The comics don't have to be funny; they can simply recount a story, frame by frame. Ask children to write what is happening in each frame on the lines below and have both characters in the frame speak dialogue that supports the storyline. Explain that since space in the bubbles is limited, the written words should just support the narration, not tell the story. Remind students to write small and concisely. This takes some planning and forethought. If possible, have children outline their ideas on a separate piece of paper and briefly conference with you, a parent volunteer, or a peer for approval. Once edited, children can copy their three sentences onto their comic strip and write the title on the line above the frames. Have them write their name on the bottom, centered line. Trace over the completed writing with a black, felt-tip marker.

For their drawings, have children work in pencil first. Once you approve their sketches, have them outline their drawings with a black felt-tip marker, and then color completely with colored pencils. Remind them to color with heavy coverage so the finished piece bursts with color. Tell children not to color in the speech bubbles. Leave these white so they stand out and the words can be read more easily. Share completed entries and enjoy!

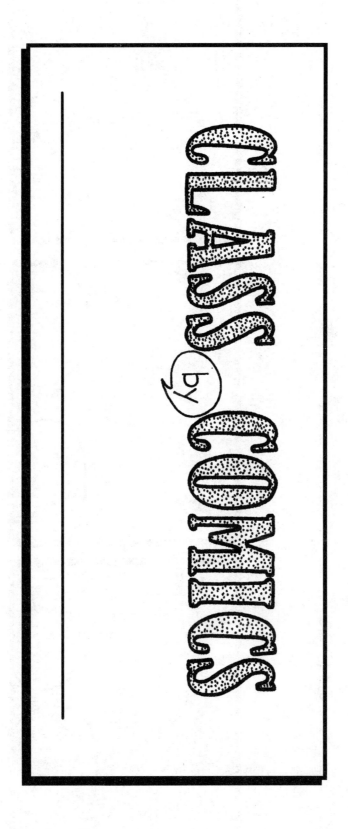

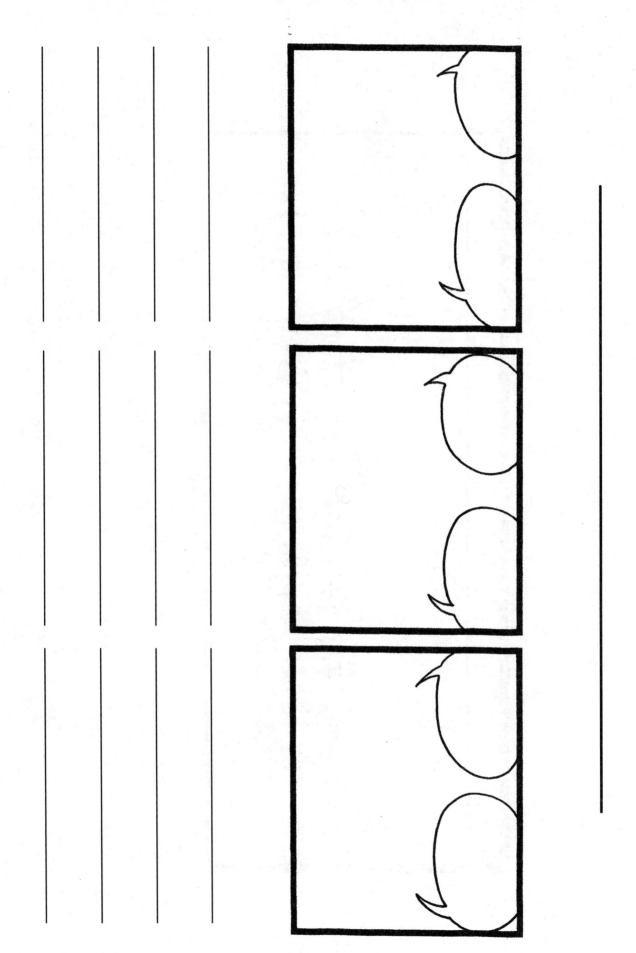